THE

TUPPER REPORT

ON SCOTTISH EDUCATION

For Sam Polson, who made an accurate forecast.

ISBN 0 9513913 05

First Published in 1988 by The Ravenstone Press,
in association with Bookspeed (distribution),
48a Hamilton Place, Edinburgh, EH3 5AV

Printed by Northern Printers, Thurso, Caithness, Scotland

THE TUPPER REPORT

ON SCOTTISH EDUCATION

With an Introduction by
THE BARON OF RAVENSTONE

CONTENTS

INTRODUCTION

Since the Sixties, voluminous official reports have enquired exhaustively, recommended extensively and pontificated pompously on every aspect of Scottish State Education and, like grotesque, ungainly toads, these reports have in their turn spawned countless progenies of discussion papers. None of them has had any effect whatever on the consumer, the Scottish public and parents, who see the system changing, crumbling, falling apart and becoming less and less effective before their bewildered and increasingly angry eyes.

This lack of communication is hardly surprising, as the reports and papers are couched in the impenetrable bureauspeak of mediocrity, an unfortunately revealing reflection on the linguistic abilities of our masters.

Tom Tupper, Headmaster of Strathmurder Secondary School — he claims to owe his position to having been taught the Masonic handshake at a Shetland Up Helly Aa — has compiled a guide that says it all, sharply. Containing everything you need to know (and never dared to ask) about Education and Schools in Scotland, his Report and illustrations are an education in themselves.

The Baron of Ravenstone

PRIMARY TEACHERS: 1. THE INFANT TEACHER

Infant teachers know more about children than any other type of educationist. They know about them because if they didn't they wouldn't be doing their job long: they'd be in an institution, or working in Presto's or in anything other than infant teaching. They have to tie the shoes, wipe the noses (and other messy parts), mop up the floor, take their pupils to lunch, tell them when it's time to go home, keep them from crying, cajole them into some sort of order out of total chaos, entertain and enthral them, and teach them things as well. Unlike any other practitioners they can't get a bit of peace by telling pupils to write a story, take out a reading book or do a project on the Romans. Nor can they treat them as a class, because each one is totally, undeniably an individual. At no time are they teaching a subject: they teach children. There are no bad infant teachers.

PRIMARY TEACHERS: 2. THE STALWART

Members of the public who think that a teacher's lot is a doddle and merely chalk and talk, know nothing about the amazing variety of activities planned, engineered and encompassed by the stalwarts of Scottish Primaries. Six months of it would be more than enough for many an able-bodied citizen, yet the stalwart does some forty years. They teach every conceivable subject, from reading to micro-computers, attempting the impossible daily as a matter of course. They mark innumerable jotters, and by the sheer force and unflagging enthusiasm of their personalities do more to enrich the cultural life of their charges than, in the majority of cases, any other human agency will ever do for the rest of their lives. If anyone deserves a medal or a Royal Order at the end of the day for services to the Nation, to culture or to the human spirit, they do. Yet except their colleagues club together for a modest presentation to mark their retirement, they're generally turned out to grass without so much as a word of thanks from the Bureaucracy.

Scottish Primary Schools always did contain a certain number of enthusiasts for Nature Study, but in the Sixties, the Trendies who seized power then sloshed it together with History, Geography and Science into Environmental Studies. Even Maths and English were, at the height of this fad, supposed to be taught as part of the Environmental Studies syllabus. The Environment had definitely arrived, and with it came the Alternative Society, Flower Power, Ecology, Green Politics, Rainbow Warriors, Animal (and Women's) Lib and Friends of the Earth. Teachers who found themselves harmlessly attracted to Nature came fully into officially approved flower, stepped right out of the closet or potting-shed, and frolicked with their classes frequently up hill and down dale, through ferny hollow and mossy grot.

The chief educational benefit of this is that from an early age, it allows children experience of adults who are quite batty.

PRIMARY TEACHERS: 4. THE VISITING SPECIALIST

If the Divisional Education Officer (see p 75) is keen and in funds, he may try and appoint one or two weekly visiting specialists to his Primary Schools: Music, Art, P.E., Craft (previously Needlework and now "Life Skills") being the main specialities. These may be either itinerant teachers employed to visit a number of Primaries, or teachers of these subjects in local Secondary schools sent into outer darkness for one two days per week, often due to over-staffing in the Secondary.

A good, vigorous visiting specialist is a big advantage for a Primary school: at their worst, they at least allow the Primary teacher a short free period. Unlike their Secondary colleagues, Primary teachers normally have no free periods. The specialist is therefore welcome, and often plays a full part in project work or concerts and sports, although Artists, with their Bohemian attitudes to the rigidities of Regional funding, have been known to use up a whole session's paint supplies in one morning of exuberant artistic self-expression.

The secret is to merge with the paper-work.

In the past, the Scottish Headmaster or Headmistress wielded considerable power both in the school and in the community. Today he has virtually none, although his responsibilities have multiplied like rabbits. The Head Teacher must therefore be a combination of juggler, trapeze artist and conman. Or perish. He must cope daily with mountains of very distracting paperwork from a welter of official and semi-official sources — hardly any of which has relevance to the proper running of his school — and at the same time supervise staff, pupils and ancillaries, deal with the unexpected, cope with the recalcitrant pupils without touching a hair on their heads, entertain and be polite to parents, no matter how outrageous or rude, and — most important of all — he must be ever-ready to pour forth the correct flannel to official visitors.

Heads are now often selected not so much because they are proven effective educators, but because they are likely to please and not ruffle the host of bureaucrats they must communicate with. Almost all Heads are nowadays young, or youngish. Only the toughest, or smoothest, survive middle age.

PRIMARY TEACHERS: 6. THE TEACHING HEAD

In most of the smaller Primary Schools — those with a roll between one and a hundred and fifty, or thereby — the Head Teacher works full-time as a class teacher as well. This means that, in addition to the duties, skills, acts and pressures enumerated on the previous page, he or she has also to teach between one and seven classes as well, with all that that entails in correction, preparation and energy. Some Education Authorities make some allowance for this and some do not: what it means is that the Authority gets the services of a Head Teacher and a class teacher for the price of a teacher plus a part-time clerkess. Which is usually a bargain.

These educational Stakhanovites are generally living on borrowed time, if stress has a shortening effect on human life, and not a few of them have been known, under provocation, to tell bureaucrats exactly what to do with their Guidelines and forms. This, of course, serves only to reduce their chances of ever being promoted to bigger, non-teaching Headships.

NOTE: Although male Head Teachers are portrayed on these pages, there are at least as many female practitioners of this craft in Primary Schools. It's just that they move so much more quickly it's impossible to sketch them.

PRIMARY TEACHERS: 7. THE SOLE TEACHER

Despite official policy in favour of closing small schools, there remain, mainly because of insurmountable topographical reasons, a number of single-teacher schools, in remote areas and on small islands where it would be impracticable to transport the pupils to the nearest larger establishment. The theoreticians and economists emphasise the drawbacks, but a good, dedicated single teacher can make a very friendly, caring family out of her small charge, and such schools can be models of stability and quiet, purposeful progress. Conversely, a bad appointment means that children are stuck with an unsympathetic teacher throughout their Primary schooling.

In Shetland, there are still a few sole teachers who must also function as Lay Missionaries on their islands. Considering the paperwork and the energy required to cope properly with children of divers stages from 4 to 12, and the present state of religious enthusiasm throughout our island nation, only saints or martyrs need apply.

SECONDARY TEACHERS: 1. THE TRADITIONAL FIGURE

The traditional Scottish Secondary teacher is now but a legendary figure, yet there must be many members of the public still creaking about who can remember him or her. Vividly. He wore a sports jacket, which his manly, often rugby-induced, physique filled well, baggy flannels or gaberdines — corduroys in the case of deviates — a woollen pullover and no-nonsense spectacles. He believed implicitly that a decent teacher needed only three pieces of equipment, none of which set the taxpayers back a bomb: a blackboard, a box of chalk and a belt. This latter he often carried in his jacket, ready to hand for immediate use without further fuss and bother. Given these simple tools, he would cheerfully do his job and all that it entailed without girning, striking or protests. He had no qualms, and knew exactly what his status was and required, both in and out of school. He took sports practice, drama clubs, cycle tours, cricket teams, or whatever else his forte was, after school, on Saturdays, in the holidays if necessary. He knew, and had a healthy regard for his pupils as immature learners, and had neither illusions about them nor hang-ups about treating them to a whack or two with the tawse when they were naughty or remiss. His pupils called him "Flogger", knew exactly where they were with him, and learned to work hard and keep out of trouble if they wanted to make anything of themselves.

SECONDARY TEACHERS: 2. THE PINKO

Sometime in the famous Swingin' Sixties, they officially threw away the patterns and moulds for the traditional Scottish teacher (see previous page) and adopted instead a policy of letting a Hundred Flowers Bloom, provided all the flowers were pink ones. Authority, Discrimination, Elitism, Conformism and Middle Class Values had to be overthrown, and tilting at these phantasmagorical windmills became the principal purpose of the Trendies, from the Inspectorate downwards. Education in the structured, traditional sense became a dirty word — in some places, the only dirty word. The concept of a ladder, up which the pupils climbed from one steady rung to the next, was officially scrapped. In its place came the Morass, in which all wallowed, gloriously equal.

This Revolution was accomplished not by a spontaneous rising of the masses — few revolutions are ever that — but by being imposed from the top. It could never have happened otherwise.

SECONDARY TEACHERS: 3. THE UNION MILITANT

There was a time, admittedly rather a long time ago now, when the E.I.S. was a douce, professional association that was as reluctant to make a controversial statement, let alone a blatantly political one, as a seminarian in a Trappist order. With the coming of Trendy Times however, the Pink Flowers thrived and in many instances became full-grown Red Hot Pokers. These sturdy blossoms flourish particularly well in certain soils, particularly in Lanarkshire, Glasgow, Lothian and West Fifeshire, until in several swathes and lush parterres of the educational garden they have run riot together, blotting out a host of smaller, tenderer plants that used in former times to hold their own in countless nooks and crannies, rock gardens and shady grots.

The real trouble with chucking away order and purpose in a garden is that the flowers seem to think thereafter that the garden exists mainly for them to flourish in, to fulfil their dreams as Big Red Plants. The garden has now, of course, become a wilderness, and like most wildernesses it has largely ceased to be either productive or effective, except as a haven for wildlife.

As there were no longer any accepted professional standards or models, it is hardly surprising that a rich variety of teaching methods and techniques have resulted. Some teachers, having generally, at least in retrospect, enjoyed being teenagers and carefree students, see no anomaly in refusing to mature beyond that, perhaps feeling secure in thus identifying themselves with their pupils. They can dodge responsibilities better and claim to be in closer rapport with The Kids. They frequent discos and denounce teaching as a drag.

Perversely, pupils — who have learned to put up with just about anything from teachers — are irked by this type, especially if he/she is pushing 23. There are Professional Teenagers in their late forties — relics of Flower Power and other ancient civilizations — but most pupils regard these tolerantly as harmless geriatric freaks.

Successful teachers always did employ considerable acting skill, but with the scrapping of official standards, many have substituted their favourite roles for the repudiated professional image. Hence the classroom Trotskys, Lenins and Disco Queens on the preceding pages.

The Star Turn teacher, who puts a great deal of energy and even talent into his daily presentation can be a very diverting and welcome change from serious study. There can be no questioning his own belief that he would probably be better on telly. Or anywhere else.

He is no new phenomenon, however: the Star Turn teacher has a long pedigree.

SECONDARY TEACHERS: 6. THE PART-TIME FARMER

A role frequently espoused by non-urban teachers, for want of any serious professional purpose, is that of the farmer. The farm usually amounts to a modest smallholding with but a few sheep or goats, but it can be made to yield profit, not least in terms of image. The battered Landrover, the green wellies, check shirt and mouldy body-warmer can be considerable props in times of crumbling self-esteem, vanishing professional pride and diminishing financial incentives.

Serious practitioners of this art can hope to retire early, and devote themselves to something richly satisfying.

Like the Star Turn (page 17), the Lady Bountiful is a long-running institution in Scottish schools and no mere by-product of the Sixties. She has generally married some person of quality, landowner, prosperous farmer or bonnet laird, and returned to teaching either *to keep herself from turning into a complete vegetable* or to help pay for the second Range Rover.

At her best, the Lady Bountiful can provide a welcome splash of alien culture to the school, a splendid hydrangeal blue among the prevailing pinks. At her worst, she treats everyone else as if she were doing them a favour merely by deigning to come amongst them. For her young charges, she is a creature from another planet. But then, so are almost all the other staff.

Variations on the Lady Bountiful include the Miss Jean Brodie and the Dame Edith Sitwell.

The preceding types have at least some virtue of singularity and noticeable distinguishing features. Each of them has dealt with professional problems peculiar to the Age in a way best fitting his/her own natural bent. The curse, however, as any healthy fourteen year old will aver, is not the weirdo but the bore, droning on forever in a virtually unchallengeable vacuum. Even the most undisciplined yobbos succumb at last to his effortless banality, his untiring pursuit of heavy, overpowering pedagogic stodge.

He has been on the go since schooling was first invented, but now, like the other types, he has freer range to perfect his act.

The sensitive practitioner who can't get his act together and keep it going for five days a week before a live audience, may have recourse to artificial stimulants and tranquillizers. This, again, is nothing new, although it has so increased with stress and professional uncertainty that certain Regional Authorities enclose little pink leaflets in teachers' pay packets at appropriate times of year — such as Yuletide — advising them of what they should do if they turn unaccountably into alcoholics.

Discipline is the main problem, that daily golgotha they have ever to face: self discipline, that is.

SECONDARY TEACHERS: 10. THE PROBATIONER

Students and young teachers freshly let out to practise their skills have always been fair game for jokers, so there's not much new going on in this sphere of academic activity, except that, of course, pupils can get away with more now than in the past, though older readers with memories as yet unclouded by the warping prejudices of old age may have their own reasons to doubt this, for even when retribution took the form of an immediate belting, this did not deter the dedicated prankster. Conversely it can be argued that today's pupils can be more understanding and sympathetic to the young and unfledged.

Whatever way you look at it it takes courage.

Partly because old teachers are seldom seen militating in public, partly because of the high level of suicide, premature senility, fag-smoking and other forms of early retirement, people are unaware that in many Secondary schools ancient reptilian pedagogues still lurk, in Science cupboards, English departments and the like, relics from the Age of Monster Reptiles. Such bloodless creatures can exercise the power of the living dead over their horrified pupils, for many of whom they are the real-life embodiment of video nasties. For the Stiff, even the punk and the Christmas Leaver will hand in homework more or less on time, and sit in tremulous silence.

Any real teacher is an enthusiast, as pupils know instinctively. It's something you either have or you haven't. A real professional knows how to keep his enthusiasm going and works hard at it. The pusillanimous get discouraged early, and thereafter it's going to be a long, unpleasant struggle all the way.

Not all enthusiasts are Artists (and not all Artists are enthusiasts, unfortunately). There are enthusiasts in Computers, Maths, History and many other unlikely subjects. They all tend to be impervious to the frequently appalling conditions they work in, and a school with a lot of them just has to be a good one. Conversely, a teaching staff without enthusiasm means a pretty foul school.

Enthusiasm, the essence of the decent teacher (see previous page) beats like a wild metronome at the heart of many a Music specialist, few of whom could possibly survive without it. To start a Monday morning with a double period of Singing with 35 huge, beastly louts demands a great deal more than an LRAM and an interest in Wagner's Ring. To hear such unpromising material come to heel and warble their way through a morning of arpeggios and Lily the Pink at the behest of a frail female seated at a battered piano is to know that all is not yet lost with European Civilization.

Out are the *My Love's an Arbutus* and *Oh For the Wings of a Dove* schmalz of past schooldays. In are pop lyrics, vulgar ballads and reggae rhythms. If ever there was an argument for payment by Performance, this is it. A very skilled operator, this one.

Gone are the days when boys who were deemed incapable of Latin spent four years trying to make a dovetail joint in some lowly cellar next the boiler room. Whilst History and English specialists may still get away with trotting out to the same old material, Woodwork and Metalwork have been liberated, and pupils both male and female are given every encouragement to be creative from the start, turning out wood sculptures, ashtrays, wheel barrows, coffins, and personal adornments ranging from rings and bracelets to useful chains and suits of armour. Suites of furniture made from modern materials (chipboard and staples) compare very favourably with similar items available on easy credit at all High Street furniture stores, whilst items made of real wood have all the unique value of a craftsman-made item.

P.E. (formerly P.T.) staff have always had an easier row to hoe than their colleagues, simply because, apart from a tiny minority of professional asthmatics and obese malingerers, most pupils are generally more in favour of playing games and running about than sitting at desks and working. They have done comparatively well out of the Trendy Times emphasis on individual fulfilment, health and fitness. The best of them, unlike colleagues in other disciplines, set a personal example which cannot fail to appeal to young people.

SECONDARY TEACHERS: 16. MR. NINE TO FOUR

Traditionally, and of necessity, teachers do not stop working when the pupils run out at the final bell. There's all that marking for a start, and nowadays, in theory, there's the curriculum development, staff meetings, departmental discussions and preparation, not to mention after-school activities like sports, clubs and parents' meetings.

Work to Rule put a stop to all that for Union hardliners, and for many another who saw it as a good excuse to jack it in anyway. There always were the Nine to Four practitioners who regard the school day as an unwarrantable interference with their private lives. Recent developments have merely given them a good excuse: solidarity with the Workers' Struggle.

Tatty though most staffrooms look to the uninitiate, with their half-finished mugs of cold tea, overflowing ashtrays and piles of jotters left around all over the place, they are nevertheless havens of refuge and brief relaxation for the practitioners. If they're lucky, they'll also be places for therapeutic, communal moaning about the shortcomings of divers pupils, the Education Authority and, possibly, the Head Teacher, Not infrequently, wit, repartee and gossip are here exchanged to the mutual good and relief of all.

This blessed if brief relief can be drastically shattered by the intrusive bore. Not all bores are male, but the worst probably are, especially if they have some sort of promoted post.

Crofting, as everyone knows, is not economically viable without a subsidiary occupation, and crofters being a particularly astute breed of person have long been accustomed to combining their mystic agrarian skills with all manner of financially more remunerative callings in order to preserve their unique and time-honoured lifestyle. Fishing, roadwork, postal delivering, ferry crewing, bus driving, oil rigging and the provision of bed and board for the tourists are only a few of the better known elements in this precarious but evergreen mosaic, and for those who were pushed at the school and managed somehow despite life's manifold distractions to stay the course at a university, there is the teaching.

Such indeed is the very ideal occupation for a crofter, providing not just necessary finance but a fine balance of academic and rustic toil, plus time off in the summer for a host of essential duties like haymaking and sheep rooing. Add to this that Crofter-Teachers mostly inhabit remote and glorious islands — with remote and glorious remoteness payments and island allowances — and it can be seen that this species — now perhaps rarer than it once was — is amongst the wisest and happiest not only of the profession but of the whole human creation. Long may it thrive.

Sometime in the Sixties, the Unions finally managed, for justifiable professional reasons, to have the employment of Non-Certificated teachers banned. This meant an end to Authorities employing anyone they chose — defrocked vicars, failed students and a host of other persons without training — to teach in schools.

It also meant, unfortunately, the end of the line for a number of excellent people with valuable skills in the big wide world but no teaching certificates, including retired Sea Captains who taught Navigation, and ladies with a lifetime of skill in hand-knitting. Most of these people brought, as well as their expertise, a welcome whiff of reality into the schools that were lucky enough to have their services.

Other Extinct Species include the Lady Adviser — who dealt single-handed with all the Girls' Problems without fuss, and who has since been replaced by a host of Guidance Staff — and the Latin Teacher. Whatever happened to all of them?

Time was when being the Headmaster of a Scottish Secondary school could be a very rewarding, well worth aiming for target, and older readers will probably remember such figures, justly respected in their schools and in their communities. It was never an easy job, but today it is a completely impossible one, and the only people who want to do it tend to be cast in a different mould from the magisterial paternalists of the past. It's impossible for a number of reasons: the schools are now so big that the Head barely knows his own staff let alone his pupils; there is no effective, straightforward disciplinary system apart from force of personality — a force which cannot possibly be effective when the person concerned is only vaguely known, and a force, too, often lacking in many practitioners; pinko and other disaffected staff can be deliberately obstructive to the Head's authority; parent power is worshipped by the Trendies; paperwork, ever monumentally burgeoning, is all. The faceless nonentity rules.

Many teachers aver that the best Head is the absent Head: the guy who spends most of his time away on committees. Deputy Heads and Assistant Heads, having more manageable duties, are often the only people with effective control.

TEACHER TRAINING

The most fatuous, useless professional person a Secondary teacher is ever likely to meet in the course of his career — with the exception of Advisers, of course — is the College of Education lecturer. Not everything that is wrong with the Scottish educational system is their fault, but closing down their establishments tomorrow would be a major step in the right direction. Their sole purpose appears to be to bore and exasperate graduates with a lot of self-fancying trendy taradiddle, and start them off on their career with the distinct, and unfortunate, impression that they are enlisting in a regiment of ninnies. The last thing they are capable of doing is providing effective and sensible training in the very demanding craft of teaching. Such practical hints and confidence the trainee does acquire he gets from experienced practising teachers.

EXITS: 1. RETIREMENT

To the young, Retirement is only the last short stop before the terminus, but for the time-expired teacher it can be the gateway to life itself, the start to an eternally delayed entry into all you ever wanted to do with your life, talents and energies, and never had the time for before.

Leaving school at sixty or sixty five has the same effect as leaving it at sixteen or eighteen: liberation, all the more sweet because so long delayed, all the more valued because you know you're not going to fritter away the rest of your life in mis-spent youth. Many, of course, fall before they get to the final gate, but it is common to find that those who do get there take on a new lease of life, a pubertal spurt. Ancient, creaking pedagogues who've been suffering for years go into retirement and suddenly become fit and well, taking up new ways, activities and enthusiasms. The dead arise, the lame walk, the blind see. The crabbit come out of the closet.

EXITS: 2. FLIGHT

For many, the distant lure of sun-kissed foreign strands combines with an overpowering desire to get away from it all to take them off on the next available flight to distant parts. Some disappear forever on cruises, some sell all that they have and go to live in Sunny Spain or France, some metamorphosing into garrulous sages in out-of-the-way tavernas. Few wish to be reminded of their murky past.

Others settle for a full dose of the domestic bliss, determined grimly to enjoy what they have spent most of their lives paying for to building societies, banks and other loan sharks. This way they can still meet old colleagues, frequent the same hostelries and continue to chunter along in the same grooves but without the hassle. They might even, if the boredom gets too much, go the extreme of joining the nearest branch of the Ex-Teachers Organization, a legion of the lost if ever there was one. Hedge clipping, lawn mowing, rose pruning and other trivial pursuits take over where marking, examining and report writing left off, filling the declining years with a host of small worries and minor triumphs, almost as if one were still at work.

EXITS: 4. EARLY RETIREMENT

Teachers' Unions get more mail about Early Retirement than any other topic, not by any means all of it coming from old stagers. Only a few ever leave teaching under their own steam, and this, considering the vast numbers who say they want to do so, is often taken as proof that teaching is the only job they could do.

In the Sixties and early Seventies, when dropping out was generally regarded as cool (and when economics seemed of secondary importance to fulfillment), some did leave and take up alternative life styles like craft work, get-away-from-it-all crofting — no connexion whatever with real crofting (see page 30) — and a variety of menial jobs on oil related projects. Many of these have now begged their way back in at the school gates, and of those who haven't, only a few have struck it any richer. Those few, those happy few, are the envy of all.

In past ages, the "Stickit Minister" often ended up as a parish dominie, instilling a proper fear of the Lord and the Wrath to Come, not to mention an immense amount of Classical knowledge, into the youth of many a remote and otherwise barbarous village.

Nowadays, whilst no one who isn't properly and officially qualified can become a teacher, virtually anyone can set up as a Minister of Religion, and it is not unknown therefore for teachers to escape the rigours of the classroom by this route. Whether they thus jump from the frying pan into the fire is not for us to say, but for the long-suffering teacher's spouse — a sub-species richly deserving a Royal Order of some sort — it can mean yet another considerable sacrifice.

Many teachers, however, marry others of their own kind — and a teaching couple can make quite a decent living. It also means, on a more personal level, that they know what to expect.

EXITS: 6. THE FINAL SOLUTION

We live in an age when electronics has devalued fame, but people will still be telling their offspring fabulous stories about their best, or worst, remembered teachers long after today's TV superstar has slid without trace from the bemused memory of the impressionable viewer. To spend forty years educating the young of several generations just *has* to leave something more behind than a dot on the silver screen, and the real practitioners who put all the zest and enthusiasm into it, and make the reluctant realise some of their true potential are remembered long after they're gone. Their effect for good is incalculable, and something that should be seriously considered by those tempted to see nothing but the frustrations and repetitions.

The Kings and Prime Ministers get into the History books, but it is the teachers that enter the memories and hearts of the people.

PUPILS: 1. PLAY GROUP

Not content with having their offspring educated from below the age of five — European countries do not start formal schooling till the age of six (seven in Scandinavia and the USSR) and arguably produce a better educated pupil — Scottish parents often carry and wheel their toddlers to Play Groups to give them an even earlier start in life's great rat race. The majority undoubtedly do so from mixed motives, parts of the mixture being fashion and the need to be seen to be keeping up with it, (the Scots must always follow the English), and convenience: it's easier to take one's infants there and have a nice natter with other mums than attempt to do the job oneself.

Play groups vary enormously, according to the ethic of those in charge. They can be merely disorganised pandemonia where the young learn they can get away with murder in concert with their peers. They can also be an excellent means of socializing young children and instilling some of the rudiments of education.

Most experienced Infant teachers would prefer it if parents stuck in the first instance to teaching their offspring how to do up their shoes and garments.

PUPILS: 2. THE INFANT

Starting school is probably a lot less traumatic nowadays than it used to be, and most of the tears shed when that fateful day finally arrives come from mums' eyes.

The Infant Room of a Scottish Primary school always was a magic sort of place. The informality of the teacher and the room, the encouragement given to parents to come in, and the positive effects of play groups have all helped to blur the finality of the first few days. Perhaps if the little inmates could understand that an eleven year stretch lay ahead of them — with no time off for good behaviour — there would be a lot more trauma and wrist slashing. But children of this age are blessed with a total unawareness of both the future and the past. Every day is an eternity. They are soon absorbed in the endless fascination of the group they have joined.

PUPILS: 3. ROLE LEARNING (f)

Some of the most appalling people in education today are going around insisting that schools make no distinction between male and female pupils, and ought to be positively combating any influences that help boys grow up boyish and girls grow up into little women. The lengths these freaks and perverts would go to if given the full backing of the Authorities is plain from their successes in the great Southland — the model, as always, we must all follow.

So far, despite everything, Scottish Primary pupils remain on the whole perfectly impervious to the trend, and although it is no longer legal for a school to arrange to have its little girls learn needlework while the boys do handwork or play football — (how many of our older readers suffered permanent psychological, sexual or social damage from such iniquities?) — girls still play with girls and boys with boys. This is basically because the whole purpose of going to school, for a child, is not to gain academic or parental praise, but to get, maintain or improve one's place in the peer group. All adults, no matter how well liked, are therefore irrelevant.

This is an example of how God protects children from the age they live in.

Boys will be boys, being unfortunately ignorant of the divers sections and subsections of the Sex Discrimination Act, and will take considerable delight, generally, in taking part in divers manly sports they see on telly. Here they learn as much about life as girls do standing yakking in their allotted cloakrooms. It is not at all unknown for girls to be included in Primary football teams from time to time, particularly in small rural schools where there may not be enough senior boys, but, for some aberrant reason, most little girls do not seem to like being hacked in the shins or hit in the face with a size four football inflated to regulation firmness. The Trendies have a lot of work still to do here.

The healthy growing child gradually learns that he is held responsible for the consequences of his own actions, and is quick to comprehend the corollary to this: that he must vigorously deny the action was his in the first place. This is well encapsulated in the classic Scottish claim: *It wisnae me, it wis him/her/it.*

As understanding of virtually the whole of Scottish History depends on mastering this simple apophthegm, its importance in the upbringing of children can hardly be mistaken.

PUPILS: 6. TOP PRIMARY

By the time pupils reach Primary Seven, their teachers often wonder if some of them have heard anything at all in their previous seven years, and they often sweat blood trying to make good many of the deficiencies. There are always pupils at this level who still do not appear to know the capital of Scotland, how to spell Britain, what eleven elevens are, what a Jacobite was, which way up to hold a blank map of Europe, how to use a protractor and a lot of other basic matters their teachers have laboured long to impart unto them, the better to equip them for The Life to Come (i.e. Secondary).

Whilst there are probably always a few who will never master such pearls of information and applied technology, many fail to grasp them in Primary because they just aren't mature enough to see their significance. During the next two years, they will probably come to enlightenment, as most Secondary schools spend a great deal of time in their First and Second Year classes doing what has already been done in Primary.

Whilst there has long been talk about establishing proper links between Primary and Secondary schools, and thereby improving the prospects of what is pompously termed the Ten to Fourteen Age Group, in reality these hardly exist at all, and pupils leaving Primary Seven have to jump for themselves across an unbridged chasm. Some take it in their stride, some fall flat on their faces, some disappear forever, and for most it presents considerable problems.

One reason no bridge has been built is the likelihood that if one were constructed the teachers on either bank would rush onto it like the opposing forces at Stirling in 1297. Certainly, there is little love lost between Primary and Secondary teachers. The latter regard the former as mere play school baby minders, know absolutely nothing about the immense breadth of work that goes on in most Primary schools, and spend, or waste, a lot of time in First and Second Year classes teaching pupils what most of them already know. Primary teachers, on the other hand, often regard their Secondary colleagues as layabouts with lots of free periods and only one subject to teach. They also tend to blame them for the unfortunate fact that their nice former pupils soon turn into nasty truculent teenagers once they get up to Secondary school. If Scottish education weren't in a gutless, paper-shuffling shambles, this is a gap that would not just have been bridged, it would have been filled in long ago, preferably with the bodies of advisers, inspectors and bureaucrats.

PUPILS: 8 THE WIMP

For the pupil who has taken his Primary education seriously, worked hard and developed some satisfaction from it — which means the majority, even today — starting at many of our Secondary schools is like stepping overboard into uncharted and very unruly depths. Here, far from being regarded as a hard-working, reasonably reliable person, he is mocked and picked on as a wimp — sometimes not only by pupils. His parents, having conscientiously studied the obligatory School Handbook distributed as the Law demands by the new school, may have kitted him out in the school uniform mentioned therein, leaving the child to discover for himself that no one actually wears the thing there and anyone that does so out of ignorance is picked on from day one. In some places any child who attempts to take lessons seriously is the object of continuous mockery or bullying.

The system that once regarded Perseverance and Hard Work as the great Scottish virtues has been so traduced by Trendies and others that today the innocent new entrant is likely to discover that the nutter is the norm.

PUPILS: 9. THE JUNIOR NUTTER

Boys have always been given to mischief, but it is only in comparatively recent times that some have been able to make it into a lifestyle and get away with it 24 hours a day. In past ages, it had to stop at the school gates, and generally at the door of the family home as well. Now, many parents have given up moral responsibility and substituted entertainments and other bribes, like decadent Romans. The school, deprived of its chief deterrent, has little effective sanction against the determined nutter, who knows he can get away with it at home as well. Teachers, Guidance staff, Assistant Heads and Deputy Heads waste endless hours filling in paper to give the impression they are doing something about their nutters, all of it totally ineffective and counterproductive. The vast size of most of the schools is also clearly to blame: none of the staff knows the pupils in the first year or two — despite copious and painstaking reports sent up by their Primary schools — and as they dodge about every forty minutes or so from one stranger to another the potential nutter cannot fail to seize his opportunities. In the Primary on the other hand, even the nutter has to remain all day long under the eye of one teacher, who knows him well, and probably his parents and grandparents as well.

The Trendies and Pinkos of the Great Reforms of the Sixties having destroyed the ladders and the ordered, uniformed hierarchies of pupils, today's officially disordered rabble has substituted its own uniform, complete with such libertarian insignia as swastikas, steel studs, Iron Crosses and jackboots.

A Junior Nutter, by application and diligence at his craft, can rise to be a Yobbo, a menace, a thug, a playground bully and a classroom exhibitionist.

Thus in the brave new world of Trendy Times, these pupils are often the actual leaders, protected by loony legislation and European Courts of Justice, whilst their victims, from teachers to the well-behaved, sensibly brought-up, Christian, Jewish or Moslem child, have become the outcasts, the defenceless, the ones Authority is pleased to be powerless to protect.

Perhaps it is only a short time till such will have to wear yellow stars and be herded into cattle trucks for re-education. The Yobbo Rules O.K. in many schools, no matter what the official handbook tritely trots out. He has inherited his power from the Permissive Society.

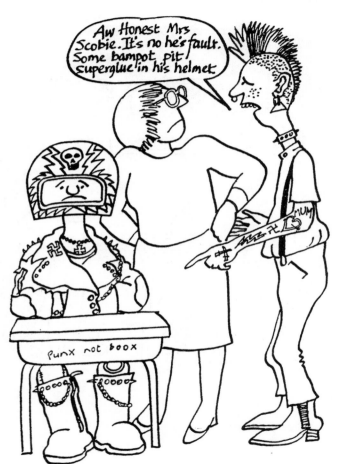

Before the great Liberalisation, it was universally recognized that not all children at Secondary schools were capable of following the same course. So, sensibly, they were streamed on entry into classes A to F, or whatever, the top classes, A and B following an academic course and those lower down following a modified one of one sort or another. Contrary to the activists' lying propaganda, the system was never rigid, and transfer from one class to another, up or down, went on all the time — as many older readers will have cause to know for themselves. Many dedicated, fine teachers chose to teach those lower stream classes as their career, and got considerable success at it.

Since the revolution, "Modified" and "Streaming" have been made into obscenities. Instead of being in classes where one could compete with one's peers on a roughly equal level, random selection rules, and everyone must do the same course, so that, for example, pupils who ought to be spending a lot of time just learning under patient guidance to read and write in normal English, **must** do French, Maths, Science and numerous other things which they cannot possibly get the hang of.

This may be Liberalization but it is not Education.

PUPILS: 12. THINGS ARE NOT ALWAYS WHAT THEY SEEM, FORTUNATELY

The young have always shocked the old: the old have always held that standards have grossly deteriorated during their lifetime. The sight and sound of some of today's school pupils is enough to make the elders of the tribe move automatically into diatribe.

Yet they have a lot more to cope with, these pupils at liberated, undisciplined, anti-learning schools than the elders had in their well-ordered, soundly taught, secure and uniformed schooldays. To cope requires a lot of maturity, tolerance and realism, and to succeed still needs a great deal of hard work.

PUPILS: 13. THE YOUNG ROTARIAN

Just as the Junior Nutter can graduate as a Bampot or Heed Banger, so the Wimp can end up a Young Rotarian, given a lot of parental determination and personal dedication. Most First year wimps give it up quickly under pressure from their peers, and thereafter become nutter-fodder, conforming more or less to the prevailing anti-school ethic and lacking any recognizable moral lead from teachers to fight back.

What it all boils down to is that the great egalitarian Revolution of the Sixties and Seventies, by which all were to have equal educational opportunities, has spawned schools where it's almost entirely those pupils with consistent parental pressure and back-up who manage to emerge with anything remotely marketable. The rest, denied the ladders and sensible, patient pedagogy they should have had, become uneducated and unemployable. It is hardly surprising that they are disruptive.

PARENTS: 1. THE TRADITIONAL

This disappearing species would like to know whit the ****** **** they think they're doing nowadays letting children get away with anything and not giving them a good belting when they deserve it. She looks back on a time when she herself was disciplined at regular intervals and never any the worse for it. She is not basically concerned with the learning content — and may freely confess that she was a bit of a blockhead when she was at school herself — but she thinks it's the school's job to educate her children and everyone else's, and to get them to work hard so that when they leave they will get a job and not become layabouts, junkies, sex freaks or perverts. She thinks that's why she pays taxes and rates.

Anyone who makes a habit of attending Parents' Evenings or Shows of Work in Primary schools has heard the oft-repeated *It wisnae like this when ah wis at school,* usually accompanied by a bemused wag of the head. Depending on the school and the quality of work displayed, the speaker can mean either (a) *We had to do right work not this playing about,* or (b) *We had a right miserable, boring time, doing ink handwriting with steel nib pens and getting hit over the head with a slate, and this is a whole lot better.*

Whichever way it's meant, there's certainly a lot of truth in it as far as Primary schools are concerned, but does anyone, Mum or Granny, ever say it about Secondary schools and mean (b)? Is anyone's Mum or Granny even allowed to see what actually goes on in a Secondary school? Would they be safe?

PARENTS: 3. MODERN

Modern, i.e. Trendy, parents are not nowadays all incomers, as the whole history of the nation is the history of copying the trends from the south of the border. Naturally, they expect schools to be as trendy as they are themselves, and in this way they are wholly supported by the bureaucrats, yapping hard at everyone's heels to impress their masters or their gods with their up-to-dateness.

Not that Modern is all wrong any more than Traditional was wholly good. Modern parents are often more actively concerned, and rightly, about the content of their children's education than their predecessors. It's the professional Trendies who have rubbished three hundred years of Scottish education, not parents.

PARENTS: 4. CLOTHKIT DISSENTERS

See, don't get me wrong pal. Ah hev no objection tae Religious Instruction for humans. Only, We are ELVES.

The Sixties did not just see the birth of modern Scottish education as we know it, it also spawned a generous brood of freedom-loving freaks, weirdos, drop-outs, flower-people and other Alternatives, many of whom have since declined into a bran-enriched, cholesterol-free but otherwise respectable middle age.

Their spirit lives on, however, and divers happy families wander over the face of our nation, settling for short periods in the delineated areas of some lucky school, remaining just long enough to set up some unlikely craft industry in a derelict croft, byre, barn or council premises — with generous assistance from the HIDB — before moving their bemused children on elsewhere. Their Pupil Record Folders are more or less permanently in the post between one Region and another. It is not unknown for such families to disappear into mountains, fairy knolls and uninhabited islands.

PARENTS: 5. MAN OF PRINCIPLE

Scottish education is in the mess it's in because at a fairly crucial time sufficient people were prepared to accept what the Trendies had to say and let them get on with it. Traditional principles were out of fashion so the majority of doubters shut up and accepted. As a result, anyone who is prepared to refuse to go along with it now, twenty years later. is regarded as a crank, an outdated relic, a narrow-minded bigot, and he'll certainly be in a very tiny minority.

Yet anyone who has had the privilege of hearing the opinions of, for example, a conscientious parent from a Highland Free Church or Free Presbyterian Church congregation, knows that such people can speak with the authentic voice of the real Scottish tradition in education that will not accept modern standards as right. Such parents would like to know why the Roman Catholics (God bless them) and now, apparently, the Moslems — not to mention the English with their Church Schools — have their own state-funded schools, but Scottish Protestants, who set up Scottish education in the first place, do not.

PARENTS: 6. THE CLAIMANT

The role of the school as educator is distinctly subordinate, in some parents' view, to its principal *raison d'être:* somewhere to dump the brats and get all their needs provided by other people who get paid to do so. Such parents complain if their children get head lice, because the nurse hasn't checked their heads frequently enough and doused them with Prioderm. They complain about lack of variety in the free meals. They shove their children out of doors long before school opening time, summer and winter, often without breakfast, and let them run around the streets or slump endlessly in front to the telly till long after bedtime. They don't help with homework because it's not their job to educate kids, and they have wee Rambo's ears pierced and plugged with gold studs, but keep him off school until they get a grant to buy him an anorak.

PARENTS: 7. THE P.T.A.

PTAs, one of the countless blessings to have come into the land from the U.S.A. via England, can be, like the Pickwick, the Owl and the Waverley Pen, great boons. There is no denying that greater parental involvement in the educational process has much to commend it.

Problems can arise however, when the PTA is, as not infrequently happens, run by and on behalf of parents who are not typical of the majority. In rural areas, they can undoubtedly be fronts for the dreaded White Settlers — though whether these intrepid people are rightly to be dreaded or warmly to be welcomed as actively reversing the process whereby the educational machine has removed generation after generation of the intelligent from the Scottish countryside and left only the dull, the feckless and the improvident, is outside the scope of this work.

Be that as it may, PTAs do tend to be run by members of the chattering classes. They can also give any school a lot of free vigour, a rare infusion of fun, and a lot of much-needed cash.

NON-TEACHING STAFF: 1. THE JANITOR

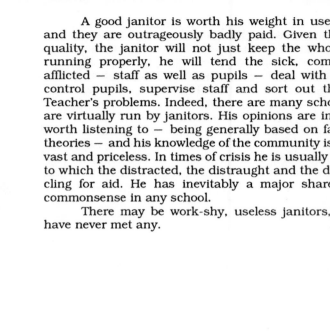

A good janitor is worth his weight in used fivers, and they are outrageously badly paid. Given the basic quality, the janitor will not just keep the whole place running properly, he will tend the sick, comfort the afflicted — staff as well as pupils — deal with visitors, control pupils, supervise staff and sort out the Head Teacher's problems. Indeed, there are many schools that are virtually run by janitors. His opinions are invariably worth listening to — being generally based on facts, not theories — and his knowledge of the community is usually vast and priceless. In times of crisis he is usually the rock to which the distracted, the distraught and the disgusted cling for aid. He has inevitably a major share in the commonsense in any school.

There may be work-shy, useless janitors, but we have never met any.

The clerkess, often part-time, is like the Janitor: a grossly underpaid person who usually knows a lot more about the running of the school than the professionals, and keeps the whole paper-heavy operation running efficiently. Without her expertise, suicide rates would rise steeply amongst senior staff. In an age when whole vast Regions — we use the word **vast** advisedly — are run on the principal *Keep your paperwork up to date, and the rest will look after itself,* her knowledge of form finding, form filling and the whole paper panoply of the Regional, sub-Regional and District officialdom allows others to sleep easier at nights and avoid, or postpone, heart attacks. Like the Janitor, her knowledge of the local community and her commonsense in a world of comparative madness can make her a source of stability and comfort, particularly for the Head Teacher.

Elderly readers who can recall, with queasy unease, the School Dinners of yester-year — the plates of greasy mince followed by greyish sago with, if you were lucky, a small dollop of Shieldhall Mixed Fruit jam in the middle of it — would be agreeably surprised by the rich variety of foods generally on offer today to young diners. Rules governing the protein and calorific content of the dinners have been relaxed to permit the sort of food children like, plus some reasonable encouragement to eat healthy real foods as well.

This is a sound policy. It's better for pupils to scoff sausage, eggs, chips and beans, followed by yoghourt or cheese, than to half-eat a lot of nutritious mince and cabbage.

Cleaners are the stage hands of the educational roadshow, unseen during performances but essential to the operation. They start early and finish late, leaving the bit in the middle clear for the professionals and stars to sock it to the appreciative audiences.

Their job is often a daunting one nowadays, when yobbos can get away with leaving their graffiti, chewing gum, fag ends and other filth all over the place, whilst the crummy concrete buildings shoved up in the Sixties by corrupt or credulous councils, now dripping, cracked, peeling and crumbling make it often impossible to do a satisfactory job no matter how hard they try. Where they can, they generally do a first-rate job, as in those few surviving remote places where pitch pine panelling and brass door knobs still survive due to the ignorance of the Regional Architect's department or Environmental Health officials who, if they but knew of their existence, would have them ripped out in a trice as hazards counter to Regional Policy.

Horrifying tales are told in various parts of the country of little old ladies clambering aboard school buses by mistake and never reappearing. Certainly, they are no place for the squeamish, or persons with weak hearts, conservative attitudes to behaviour or objections to foul language.

Yet their drivers must be very careful to treat the young passengers with tolerance and respect, or parents will complain to officials. Booting off obstreperous louts is not nice: he/she might catch cold trying to thumb a lift — he/she certainly won't walk. Rectors and officials alike dodge the issue: discipline, the officially dirty word that any self-respecting Trendy will ever shy away from like a highly strung filly.

To be a school bus driver you need qualifications: nerves of iron, a thick skin and a belief that some Higher Power has called you to this job. No weaklings need apply.

Twenty years or more ago the visiting clergyman was usually on a hiding to nothing. He represented a fossilized church where children were bored to tears. Today, however, hardly any children or teenagers know anything at all about churches, and thus their only contact with its Message is at school. For this reason they are often prepared to listen. Unlike adults — in many schools it's the staff who refuse to have anything to do with the chaplain, not the pupils — they ask meaningful questions, and the chaplain will try and answer these, or duck them, according to his lights.

There are almost as many techniques as there are practitioners — the Sixties Trendy Vicar has long since become an established part of the scene — and all of them can make an impact. Attempts by the educational establishment to turn Religious Education into an O Grade subject are a typical dodge to substitute worthless paper qualifications for real education.

REGULAR VISITORS: 2. THE FRIENDLY NEIGHBOURHOOD POLICEMAN

Time was when a policeman would no more have appeared regularly in a school than a lion tamer. The current raised profile is partly due to the breakdown of discipline, partly to the breakdown of traditional values in society, and partly due to a desire by the police to counter the anti-police propaganda fed to the public, and to young people in particular, by a number of interested parties and wrecking groups with free and frequent access to the media.

Their job is a thankless one and, like the chaplain, the policeman not infrequently lacks the support of the school staff — a measure of the success of the Trendies.

Small children, with the innate wisdom of the very young, trust the policeman. He comes in at regular intervals to reinforce the message **Never Go with Strangers** and to teach them bike drill.

REGULAR VISITORS: 3. THE SOCIAL WORKER.

Where did they all come from? Now they're everywhere and bid fair to replace not just the chaplain and the policeman but the school as well — (Could they be any worse?).

These apostles of the great, green Humanitarian in the sky appear to be recruited from the ranks of those who spend three or four years at the taxpayers' expense studying totally vacuous subjects at universities and are then turned loose, as green and fresh as spring lettuces — (as we all were once, admittedly) — to help hardened criminals, vicious little thugs and cadging, whining, cunning members of the community. It is not uncommon for children to threaten teachers and parents with the dire warning: I'll tell my social worker on you!

Given the fact that more and more Secondary pupils are having to be fitted with sets of wallies, and even infant pupils have mouthfulls of fillings, the N.H.S. has provided funds for Teeth Ladies to visit schools at tegular intervals to teach children how to brush their teeth, and to instruct them in the benefits of healthy eating. Naturally, no one nowadays expects parents to take on such onerous responsibilities, nor to ensure that their offspring are not constantly cramming their faces with the sort of sugary rubbish that does all the damage. It's the school's responsibility: parents have no responsibilities, only rights.

The Teeth Ladies are good value for money. Pity, when the Trendies were promoting sexual promiscuity, they didn't think about the rot and decay that would cause.

REGULAR VISITORS: 5. THE NURSE

Nurses always did pay occasional visits to schools for health checks. Nowadays they are more frequently required, and that for the same sort of reason as we require Teeth Ladies: most parents have given up bothering. Head lice, unwashed and slept-in clothes, even scurvy have all made dramatic reappearances in the recent liberal decade: complaints that were generally reckoned things of the past in a modern caring society, a society that has almost none of the excuses past generations had.

BUREAUCRACY: 1. THE ADVISER, MESSENGER OF THE GODS

We now turn our attention to the Hierarchy, the great cumulus and strato-cumulus clouds and layers of officialdom that tower majestically over and above schools and their humble pupils, practitioners and parents.

To say that clouds are divorced from earthly reality is not, of course, true because they frequently pour down deluges and showers upon the humbler creation, visit it occasionally with lightning shafts of wrath, lower themselves from time to time and spread upon the earth in the form of fogs, mists and other vapours. It is also true — but seldom alluded to — that even the highest clouds are dependant upon the earth and its dreary labours for their elevated existence.

But though all this is not without truth, people generally hold the clouds to be separate, away up there, not soiled by toil, nearer to God than ordinary mortals. And so indeed do these deified creatures see themselves.

From such elevations come messengers of the gods: Advisers, assuming mere human form for this purpose, but retaining at all times their well-fed sleekness. Their function is to bring wisdom from on high, and it is a thankless task. The Adviser is wasted on mere mortals.

Advisers perhaps get a worse reputation that they deserve as they tend to be the only emissaries of the hierarchy encountered more than rarely by ordinary teachers. The odium and savage loathing they generate — being semi-divine, they never notice it — ought in fairness to be spread more evenly over the rest of Olympus.

Whilst there are advisers (we believe) who introduce good new ideas, the prevalent feeling is: (a) that they are snoopers and spies for the bureaucracy — and some of them openly avow this, using it to cajole and threaten recalcitrant teachers and Heads; (b) that they are fly wee conmen who probably do very nicely from publishers for pushing their latest ventures; (c) that they are mediocrities who never had a good or original idea in their lives, and merely swan around picking up other teachers' ideas and passing them off elsewhere as their own; and (d) that they invariably teach their grannies how to suck eggs.

Their real *raison d'être*, of course, is to keep their superiors in the clear by continually advocating the latest trends.

Occasionally summoned from his murky lair by newly appointed Head Teachers to look at a difficult child, the Psychologist is there to write copious reports in psycho-babble stating what everyone else is well aware of already. He is the ultimate quack, believing his own twaddle even when no one else does. Fortunately, he usually generates enough paperwork to bury himself — a fairly astute self-defence mechanism — so that he is hardly ever available or contactable, always *out on a case* or at a conference.

At one time the child psychologist administered various diagnostic tests to pupils at irregular intervals, which were sometimes a help in assessing progress, but since one of their Chief Priests was publicly adjudged guilty of having falsified some thirty years of his own statistics to suit some quaint little fascist and loony theory of his own devising, this function has, not surprisingly, atrophied.

BUREAUCRACY: 4. THE OFFICE

Time was when every Scottish County ran its own education. It had its own Education Committee, its own Director of Education and its own Education Office, where all the County's schools were administered and all teachers and Head Teachers were, some more and some less, known as human beings.

The majority of the public appear to believe this is still the case, and they are very far from reality in so believing. Everything local was downgraded at Regionalisation (1974) and all real power removed to the vast and anonymous Regional Headquarters — which can be over a hundred miles away — but The Office is usually still there, no longer the real centre of anything other than routine paperwork and supplies. It is the sole vestige of Pre-Regionalisation, the bottom rung of the bureaucracy's Jacob's ladder that stretches from the mud into the starry empyrean: the only place on that ladder a teacher or Head Teacher can hope to find any sort of normal friendly contact or help.

When every County had its own Education Committee, so also did each have its own Director of Education. Nowadays, Regional Directors of This, That and T'other are birds of relatively common plumage — common in the sense that there are more Directors than there used to be, not (Heaven forfend!) common in the sense of their being *vulgar* — but then, in those far-off days, there was only one Director: the Director of Education. Many of them were *gentlemen*, and those who weren't tried hard to behave as such. Many were men of considerable civilization and cultural achievement, whose offices contained bookcases with real books in them, as distinct from filing cabinets stuffed with files in bureaucratic newspeak. They were usually men who had been promoted after very considerable experience as teachers, not jumped-up administrators with, at best, only a few years in a school before joining the bureaucracy. Most important of all, they got out of their offices frequently to visit their schools, knew their Head Teachers well and personally and their teachers at least by sight and name.

And conversely, as in a Classical City State, they were known — along with their faults and peculiarities — in their County and to their people, and could not assume, like Eastern potentates, a mask of impersonal power and omniscience by living in secluded courts and hideous glass-fronted Headquarters a hundred miles away.

In place of the old County, or Burgh, Director of Education, we now have the Divisional, or Area, Education Officer. He has all the mammoth paper burdens of administering the educational establishments in his Division — (a Division, that is, of a Region, and roughly corresponding to the old County) — all the myriad problems to solve, the staffing, strikes, complaints, disciplinary enquiries, school transport, schools councils, etc., etc., etc., but he is basically a bureaucrat whose orders come down from Regional H.Q. In other words, he has all the hassle and little of the satisfaction.

Naturally, the Supreme Beings appoint people to such unedifying posts who are going to be reliable bureaucrats, not people with serious cultural interests or independent thoughts.

There are many excellent D.E.O.s. All of them are overworked. Their lack of impact as cultural giants is hardly their fault. But when Regionalisation took away the educational independence of the counties and burghs of Scotland and replaced it with bureaucrats, it dealt a major blow to civilization.

BUREAUCRACY: 7. THE REGIONAL DIRECTOR OF EDUCATION

Lord of All Being, throned afar....

At Regionalisation, the Director of Education ceased to be someone directly in touch with education and accountable to a recognizable community, and became a type of Byzantine Emperor or Oriental despot, a being so remote from the ordinary world of schools that teachers and Head Teachers — not to mention pupils — can serve their whole sentence without seeing his face. For this reason, he and his accolytes the Depute Directors and Assistant Directors may be accurately portrayed as Faceless.

As at any absolutist court, there are no doubt various high Regional functionaries, eunuchs and grooms of the bedchamber who may gain access to the Presence on bended knee or in similar servile posture, possibly even a few favoured Advisers who gain His ear fleetingly at a levée. Perhaps, too, there may even be a few chosen schools which He deigns occasionally to grace with his passing notice on his way to some more important function of Regional state, or to his barbers, hostelry or masseuse. But for the peasantry, the Head Teacher, the teachers and the rest of the messy, awkward workforce, this Domitian is known only through his incessant Directions, Guidelines and Memoranda on every subject under the sun, all of which must be read, obeyed and filed in the correctly coloured binder.

He is the Lord of All Paper, the Supreme Bureaucrat. Fail to complete your forms correctly, or treacherously dare to question any of his diktats, and he will screw your career, from his Regional Suite a hundred miles away, with the crazy, meticulous, impersonal cruelty of a Caligula.

BUREAUCRACY: 8. THE REGIONAL EDUCATION COMMITTEE

The Director is in theory the servant of the Regional Education Committee, a committee of the Regional Council. All major — and many minor — policy decisions have to be approved by this Committee, and candidates for promoted posts are generally chosen by its Chairman, in conjunction with officials, which gives that gentleman very considerable power indeed. The Chairman is the Godfather of the whole racket.

In theory, the Committee is a democratic body. In fact, any randomly selected group of citizens walking down a street or casting peats on a Saturday afternoon would be likely to be more truly representative of normal public opinion because the members of the Education Committee, being members of the Regional Council, have been selected by a notoriously unrepresentative process. The vast majority of the public don't vote in Regional Council elections (30% is reckoned a surprisingly good turnout) so they represent only a small minority of the public.

Add to these, the co-opted members representing Trade Unions, Religious denominations, etc., and you can have an Education Committee largely composed of minority representatives: vicars of minuscule congregations, leftist activists, geriatric business men who left school at thirteen, and White Settlers.

Yes, there always were Education Committees. But the old Pre-Regional ones, like the old Directors, did have some connexion with the area they were responsible for. The present system allows a group of largely ignorant, unrepresentative people power to impose radical changes and policies on places and communities they've not even visited for a day trip. And being pretty clueless themselves, the Committee members are easy prey to manipulation by smart trendies, persuasive demagogues and determined *experts*.

Responsibility for governing Scotland is delegated by the U.K. government to an appointed political satrap, the Secretary of State for Scotland. He allocates various fields of responsibility amongst Scottish M.P.s of his own party, and one of these fields, by no means the most fallow one, is Education. Thus whilst in England an ambitious politician can gain real promotion by becoming Minister of Education (whose writ does not run north of the Border), in Scotland it's generally some faceless party hack who's lumbered. This is not infrequently someone who has never been at a Scottish state school and wouldn't dream of sending his own offspring to one. The point is immaterial, as the post itself is a nonentity.

Government action in Scottish education consists in imposing financial restraints and in forcing through politically inspired reforms perpetrated in England, such as the abolition of the Junior Secondary schools. Socialist governments have been worse at this because they have often allowed trendies and theorists free reign.

In general however, those who have the power lack the nerve, the knowledge or the interest, and are content to delegate to a host of committees. They mouth platitudes, and expect their committees to act for them.

BUREAUCRACY: 10. THE INSPECTORATE

Inspectors were wisely instituted a long time ago to ensure that teachers and schools did a proper job. But since the start of Trendy Times, the Inspectorate — whose members are highly paid civil servants recruited from the teaching profession and employed by the Scottish Office — have turned themselves away from their traditional role in safeguarding the nation's education to spearheading changes invented in England and the U.S.A. And as no one with any real conviction is really in charge, they have arrogated to themselves the power to make schools adopt one trend after another in an endless process of rubbishing traditional, tried ways and substituting theories and policies that are here today and gone tomorrow.

If in all the vast antheap of muddle, stress, mediocrity, buck-passing, change and decay that is Scottish State Education today there are guilty men — as distinct from incompetent and over-burdened ones — the Inspectorate harbours them, and has been doing so for well over twenty years. They force schools to adopt policies which wisdom, experience and plain commonsense cry out against, because they can denounce them publicly with all the weight of official disapproval, and make the Regional masters look out of step with the Trend. People in power in the Regions who are unsure of themselves and don't basically know what's right and what's wrong in education any more, will do anything to avoid being exposed publicly as ninnies.

The Scottish Education Department functions by innumerable committees. These are generally composed of inspectors, advisers, staff members of Colleges of Education and a few eccentric and/or pushy Head Teachers, all selected for their conformity to the Trend whatever it happens to be at the time. The Committees and their sub-committees pour forth a never-ending deluge of Reports, Guidelines, Recommendations and Pronunciamentos, all simultaneously requiring immediate implementation. They deem every Teacher and Head Teacher to be an innovator, an expert in subjects they were never trained in, a multi-culturalist with limitless time, energy and ingenuity. Their effect is one of continuous demoralisation. No matter how hard one works, no matter how conscientiously one may try to read and understand this endless outpouring no teacher or Head can ever hope to do what it all requires. Hence, of course, they are always in the wrong, always dragging their feet.

Add the effects of S.E.D. Committee-speak to the effects and efforts of Inspectors, the Regional Education Committee and its minions (and their endless Papers, Guidelines and Regional Policy Documents as well), and the wonder is that any real teaching is still done.

One is drawn inevitably to comparing the teaching force with the Russian army in 1917: teachers are, by and large, brave, resourceful, incredibly idealistic people fighting a war with almost no real weapons. Their supposed commanders are incompetent, bland nonentities, who have helped create a society so idiotic it seems bound to no other fate than violent overthrow. No wonder many teachers are reduced to asking: When is our October? Where is our Lenin?

Scottish schools were established originally by people with firm standards directly derived from the Word of God as it was understood by Scots to relate to Scotland. Some of these early educators were no doubt time-servers, hypocrites, chancers, and greedy with it (one would not like to claim the Reformation was carried out by anyone other than human beings), but the point is that they acknowledged standards far more enduring, far more serious than the whim and fashion of the age.

A Trendy is someone who has either abandoned or never had any standards other than the smart, the political, the in-crowd consensus of his day. When such people take over the running of a nation, traditional standards based on hundreds of years of sound practice are rubbished over-night, and the trend of the day — quickly followed by the trend of tomorrow — becomes the only accepted principal for action.

One such Trend is Large is Beautiful: children in small schools are said to be deprived of all the expensive new facilities only a big school can provide. So the little schools must be closed, and the children are bussed away, by order of these unrepresentative pied pipers in gaudy raiment, to become as rootless and insecure as their masters.

Not only is this based on an educational fallacy — since the quality of education in no way depends upon the provision of expensive facilities — but it contributes largely to the death of small communities. The traditional local school allowed children time to see and experience their own community as a living, viable world, full of opportunities in its own way, not just a springboard into mass culture, a place to get out of, to leave behind for the big fun world of rat-racing.

TRENDS : 2. FAD SUBJECTS

Traditionally, the school's job was to educate children in a number of basic skills and subjects which, if properly mastered, would help and equip them for the wider world of work and adulthood. Trendy Times, however, saw this rejected as altogether too narrow, boring and not fun. The Committees got to work and soon spawned a large number of other subjects schools ought to be doing as well as teaching reading, writing and arithmetic. Suddenly all Primary schools had to be teaching French, and teachers who had no notion how to do this were made to feel inadequate and out of step.

That, of course, is how Trendyism works: teachers are made to feel permanently out of step with What is Right and Just, and have to be continually trying to master new approaches, techniques and subjects. Not only new subjects have to be taught — Health, Science, Micro-computers — but old subjects are given new names and slants. Arithmetic becomes Maths, and wee Jeannie instead of getting a confident grip on basic number work is expected (and fails) to deal with a bewildering and irrelevant syllabus of Binary, Conic Geometry, Technical and Scale Drawing, Co-ordinates, Bearings, Properties of Circles, Pythagoras' Theorem etc., etc.. English with its routine practice with simple but essential skills like spelling and punctuation becomes Language Arts — (How pompous can you get, lads?) — and self-expression replaces accuracy and literacy, with the result that significant numbers of school leavers are illiterate. History and Geography become Environmental Studies: no one knows exactly what's supposed to be covered, and teachers who probably come from far away have to get children interested in an environment many of them are only bussed into and out of every day.

TRENDS: 3. FUN NOT WORK

Hard work, perseverance, application, respect and manners were shown the door in the Sixties, and in came Fun. Spelling was Out for a start. It wasn't Fun. Discipline — always a strongpoint in Scottish schools — was Wrong. It stifles self-expression, and self-expression was what education was all about (wasn't it?). Grammar was a ridiculous, artificial survival that had never had any relevance: you didn't need to know how a car works when you learned to drive, they said. Multiplication tables hampered children's enjoyment of Maths: it was better for them (and more Fun) to play with blocks, buckets of water, bits of string and piles of sand (and they did). In History, it didn't matter what you did as long as the children enjoyed it: out went a chronological, orderly attempt to inculcate our Nation's History; in came countless bloody re-enactments in the classroom of the Battle of Bannockburn and Viking Raids, and endless projects about Ladies Dresses Through the Ages.

It was Fun. And it was Effective. The effects include vandalism, sexual promiscuity and a generation of irresponsibles incapable of coping with life's harder problems.

TRENDS: 4. DOING YOUR OWN THING.

What's sauce for the goslings is soon sauce also for the geese and ganders. If the Kids — "pupils" was Out, "scholars" inappropriate — were there to Enjoy, so were the teachers. Naturally, there were those who took it all out spontaneously and those who hung back, wondering what it was all coming to. The Inspectors and the Committees soon had willing disciples, and the traditional, staid, respectable Scottish teacher was declared a Drag, Square, Nowhere Man or whatever synonym for Fuddy-Duddy the Trend-speak of the moment decreed.

This Revolution did not occur without preparation. The preparation had been done at the universities in the Fifties, when bright and very green Scottish working-class students were led by the nose by suave Oxbridge tutors who subborned them into the ways of English Middle Class Marxism, thrilling them the while with little wine parties and elegant chatter. Thus was Scotia's heritage sold, and not for the first time either.

Trendy teachers were Fun (to begin with) and as Trendy Times came into full flush syllabus and curriculum followed perseverance and manners into the Flower Power trashcan. You could teach whatever you fancied, Man, just so long as everyone had Fun.

(Footnote: The Trend has now swung 360 degrees in favour of having everyone working according to a syllabus. *Curriculum Development* is now very much In, and Head Teachers who don't have curricula for everything from Leggo to Media Studies are being rapped over the knuckles in published Inspectors' Reports.)

TRENDS: 5. JOBS FOR THE BOYS

Like any other minority group which suddenly finds itself in power by default — like the Bolsheviks or the homosexuals for example — the Trendies naturally sought to expand their hold on the Nation's educational windpipe by rapidly promoting those who were manifestly Trendy themselves. It was the time when, to quote the present Chancellor of Oxford University, one of the Trendy Labour (now SLDP) Leaders of the Sixties, Mr Roy Jenkins, The *Permissive Society is the Civilized Society*. (He denies it now of course.) Candidates for promoted posts had to prove they were up to date, whereas previously they had been at pains to appear morally sound as well as hard working and efficient. Traditionally, teachers who had plainly departed from the straight and narrow in their private lives were unlikely to gain posts of responsibility in the education of the young, and it was generally held that a teacher ought to show some sort of decent example fit for children to follow outside as well as inside school.

Trendy Times put a stop to all that. It no longer mattered what you did as long as you knew the up-to-date answers. And had Fun.

Spend, Spend, Spend is Fun. And spending was very much part of the Sixties and Seventies ethos. Money was endlessly available. Wee girls just out of Training College who could hardly keep a Register straight were told they could requisition whatever they wanted. And they did. Old schools were torn down or condemned, and gleaming concrete and glass structures sprang rapidly from the protesting earth as contractors with feet in the Council's doors scrambled to grasp their pieces of the cake. TVs, fancy furniture, VCRs, unbelievably expensive and basically useless teaching aids, carpeted classrooms and other plastic junk became essential, as Educational Suppliers' catalogues became thicker than Family Bibles. Publishers — (God bless them) — poured out brilliantly coloured books on every possible subject, and new Reading Schemes, Maths Schemes, Science Schemes, each costing thousands of pounds per school, were pushed by Advisers, often with the terrible warning: Your school is the only one in Blankshire not using this super new Scheme! No Trendy Head worth his or her salt could possibly ignore such blandishments.

Then came the 360 degree turn around. Suddenly, there was no money left for anything. Everyone moaned and got stroppy. Concrete cracked and dripped. Smashed plate glass couldn't be replaced. The shoddy paintwork flaked and the gimcrack woodwork rotted. The carpets became saturated with damp, plasticine, chewing gum, glue and other dreadful droppings whilst cutbacks in expensive cleaning equipment made them impossible to tend. There was barely enough money left for floppy disks.

TRENDS: 7. PARENT POWER

As government funds dried up, the next Trend was to get a PTA to organize Fun Funding. Basically the idea of involving Scottish parents in their offsprings' education has a lot to be said for it. The Scots being what they are, however, there are many areas where the only people who will willingly come forward and run a PTA are the chattering classes, which usually means White Settlers, in the rural hinterland at least. These good people do have a very positive contribution to make, and it is not our intention to scorn them. They are articulate, but they are not representative.

Nor, of course, are the Trendies. The Trendy Establishment are in favour of Parent Power because, by and large, the parents who get onto PTA committees and Schools councils are themselves Trendies. They call that democracy. But when some Head Teachers conducted ballots of all the parents of their pupils on corporal punishment and found that overwhelming majorities wished it retained in some form, they were reprimanded. To listen to the Trendy parents is democratic. To seek the real majority will is populism.

Thus, as ever in Scotland since the time of the Canmores, foreigners and smart Alecs run the realm.

TRENDS: 8. BAN THE BELT

The campaign to have corporal punishment abolished in all Scottish schools was a classic example of how Trendyism rules: the smart minority used every kind of pressure, innuendo and moral blackmail to make the majority feel they were nasty old Fuddy Duddies. The classic Trendy argument, *You are the only ones persisting in this hideous, out-dated malpractice*, was used to maximum effect, and the reluctant followers — including the Unions — were cajoled by the fear of being held up to public ridicule.

Yet it is the Trendies themselves who are the odd ones out. All school education since Classical and Biblical times has made use of punishment in some form, as deterrent and as incentive, because it is dealing with immature students who must on occasion and as a matter of duty be made to work if they won't. Scotland is historically an undisciplined nation. What the Luxembourgeois or any other foreigners do is their worry. There were all sorts of ways of ensuring that abuses in the corporal punishment system were eliminated. The results of the breakdown of discipline from the Sixties onwards are everywhere to see. Ignorance, licence, vandalism, sheer crass, unchecked savagery abound. True, some children are still being educated. But these are the well-motivated, the ones with parents who will push, cajole and insist. As for the majority, the unadvantaged working class children, the underprivileged, the non-academic, — all of whom the Trendies so unctuously talk of serving — they are turned out any damned way, undisciplined, uneducated, unemployed and often unemployable.

Unlike a true revolution, the Trendy Revolution doesn't destroy its own children: it destroys other people's.

TRENDS: 9. EQUALITY MEANS LEARNING FRENCH

The greatest Trend of the Sixties, supported by every self-respecting Pink person (and by not a few who should have known better) was Comprehensivisation. Schools, they said, were perpetuating Class, and English Secondary Moderns were providing inferior education. Shirley Williams, English Education Secretary in a Labour government that comprised some of the greatest con-artists since the 1930s, decreed. And Scotland of course, despite the fact that its schools were radically different from English ones and were by tradition egalitarian, went with the Trend. Out went the Junior Secondaries and Modified classes — both of which, properly run and properly staffed, had a vital place in educating teenagers who had little taste for academic study — and all Secondaries had to be unstreamed: i.e. every class had to be of mixed ability, so that the academic high-flyers could be kept back by increasingly stroppy non-academic pupils who merely got more and more out of their depths.

Politically, it thrilled the Trendies. Educationally and practically, it began a decline in the quality of Secondary teaching: lessons had to be directed at an amorphous *middle ability range* so that pupils with real ability aren't stretched and get bored, whilst those at the lower end still don't really follow, and, not surprisingly, become discouraged and start acting up and distracting everyone else.

Comprehensivisation plus Large is Beautiful (see p 81) equals dehumanisation, cynicism on the part of both staff and pupils, and breakdown of the system.

TRENDS: 10. UNNATURAL TEXTS

It is true that some of the Trends dealt with here have, at least in the beginning, enjoyed support from apparently sensible sections of the community. As Trendy Times rolls ever onward, however, the basic silliness — (not to use a word as reactionary as Evil) — of some of these apparently unstoppable pressure groups of fashionable minority interests becomes ever plainer. Already Needlework has ceased in some Primary schools because it has been denounced to the ever-ready-to-jump-on-the-bandwagon Regional Authorities as sexist, and Domestic Science, already changed to Home Economics, is now Life Skills. In Primary schools, some excellent sets of reading books have been denounced and scrapped as Middle Class or Racist or Sexist, and publishers, having previously rushed to provide reading schemes choc a bloc with black children, one-parent families and proletarian mums busy stripping car engines while daddy changes the nappies, are now seeking to dodge flak by bringing out even newer schemes in which all the characters are animals. (Wait till the Animal Lib people get their teeth into these!)

All of which continues to cost the taxpayer a bomb. Enid Blyton is already classed by leading English Trendies with *Mein Kampf*. And who can doubt that, as the Trend Setters of Hackney and Brent have already come out in favour of homosexual families, the Broons and Oor Wullie are destined to follow Tinkerbell and Noddy into the banned book cupboards of the Trendy Nineties?

The first conclusion should be clear to anyone reading the foregoing pages. Scottish education, once the acknowledged envy of Europe and of our southern neighbour has been consistently rubbished over the past twenty years. It would be impossible to prove that it was done deliberately, but if any group had ever set about such a thing, it could hardly have succeeded better. It may suit rich countries like the USA and England to produce a generation of feckless trendies. But Scotland has ever been a poor country, and one of its greatest assets was formerly its free education system. That asset, which once afforded Scots of every rank a real opportunity to use their native talents either in or outside their homeland, has been wasted.

We prefer to think that those who are guilty are dupes and fools rather than traitors. But it is facile to say, as everyone seems to do now, that the decline in our schools is merely a reflection of the decline in the quality of society as a whole. The point is, surely, what's to be done?

Firstly, all Inspectors, members of policy Committees, Directors of Education, their Deputes and Assistants, and anyone else who has actively contributed from positions of trust and power to the present state of Scottish education — (including those now safely retired) — should be executed on the Maiden or hanged from Lauder Brig.

Secondly, all Colleges of Education — (previously called Teacher Training Colleges, but that didn't suit the pompous asses who worked in them) — should be closed immediately, and their staffs sent into internal exile to teach in the nastiest schools for the rest of their natural, or unnatural, lives.

Thirdly, all teacher training should be supervised hence-forth by the College of the Free Church of Scotland, and all candidates for the profession should be, from their first entrance into a university, under the moral and spiritual guidance of that same unique body — the only educational institution in Scotland that has retained both its vigour and its traditional values and integrity throughout Trendy Times. (One assumes that the Roman Catholic hierarchy would have some alternative proposals to make on this point.)

Fourthly, all teachers presently employed should be sent on intensive re-education courses at the hands of the same College.

Fifthly, Regionalisation of education should be abolished. Local Education Authorities should be re-established, with membership of Education Committees restricted to normal persons with children at state schools within that area.

Our schools could, properly reformed, become a vital means of regenerating the nation — (and Boy, does it need it!). Schools have been among the chief means of rekindling national identity in other European countries: in Finland, for example. Scottish schools and everyone in them are as capable as their counterparts in other formerly dependent states of being motivated by a higher and a greater aim than mere personal advancement. That aim would be a noble one: the rebirth of a people worthy and capable to reclaim their magnificent country from the degradation, betrayal and folly that previous generations have accepted at the hands of foreigners and cynics. It isn't lavish outlay of taxpayers' money such an education would require, but spirit, courage, perseverance and national dedication. These are not the virtues the Trendies

have nurtured.

Finally, whilst no reader would accuse us of Bolshevism, consider the Soviet Union. Their Revolution was not carried out by armchair pinkos. For a brief spell, between 1918 and 1924, they swept away all their traditional forms and restraints in their schools. Then they realised they had unleashed a destructive demon. From the mid-20s onwards, Soviet schools have been traditional, disciplined, hard-working places, doing their utmost to develop the young to their true potential. The hot-air theorists, the International Marxists, were shown the door in no uncertain fashion, and the aim in fact — as distinct from the theory — became the production of a great Russian nation.

Can any honest person, seeing how that nation has emerged from an illiterate medievalism to the forefront of modern technology in a matter of seventy years, doubt that Education is the Key to a nation's greatness — in our case, to a nation's very existence? It is not a key to be left in the hands of subversives and fools.